T0132504

2ND BASE

My Near Death Experience

TIMOTHY NICHOLS

AuthorHouse™
1663 Liberty Drive
Bloomington, IN 47403
www.authorhouse.com
Phone: 1 (800) 839-8640

Published by AuthorHouse 03/18/2019

ISBN: 978-1-7283-0428-1 (sc)
ISBN: 978-1-7283-0430-4 (hc)
ISBN: 978-1-7283-0429-8 (e)

Library of Congress Control Number: 2019903112

Print information available on the last page.

This book is printed on acid-free paper.

Because of the dynamic nature of the Internet, any web addresses or links contained in this book may have changed since publication and may no longer be valid. The views expressed in this work are solely those of the author and do not necessarily reflect the views of the publisher, and the publisher hereby disclaims any responsibility for them.

Credit to Peoble Divers / Peoble Photography for the images used in this book.

authorHOUSE®

DEDICATION

This book is dedicated to my daughters Kimberly Nichols and Amanda Nichols. I never talked about the thoughts in this book in their life to date. This may be their first time of hearing in depth about this. They have been supportive of me writing and being a computer and software engineer. It is different and hopefully thoughts to carry through out and cherish as they move forward in life.

INTRODUCTION AND BACKGROUND

At times we have moments in life we always remember. It may be a family event. It may be class we enjoyed. It may be some one we had fond memories with. It is a plethora of things we keep. This book reflects on an event I had in my younger years. I still have knowledge of it and thought it may be good to get it out there for the public. It is not meant for any persuasion but rather for others to think and use for knowledge and discussion.

This book is primarily around a specific incident that happened in my younger days playing baseball. For lack of better words it was a freak accident. I have rarely discussed what happened to date. It was real. And much is in my mind. I felt compelled to get this out before I leave. Hopefully it can be knowledge for others that have an interest in this. This is more commonly termed a Near Death Experience (NDE).

As for myself, I have early years of being a pretty good scholar and a career as a software and computer engineer. This body of work is not easy for me. The book is in three main parts. The first chapter is about family background and where I grew up. Sports was a central part of my family and city so there is a lot of this to absorb. Chapter Two will describe the best I can in detail about the experience itself. Chapter Three is my attempt to summarize thoughts and conclusions. Chapter 4 is reference to some scholar work relating to my incident.

This book is not intended as a medical narrative but rather one small instance of time that hopefully can contribute to further works around this subject.

CHAPTER

2

Background

Setting for this story is the upper Midwest. My hometown is Alden Minnesota. Most of my friends and family are from Minnesota and Iowa. The Nichols family is from Nichols Iowa. Two Nichols brothers founded the town of Nichols. The family branched out to the upper Midwest from there.

Duncombe and Webster City Iowa was where my Dad and Mother grew up. They were married and made their way to Minneapolis. Dad worked for Northwest Airlines and Mom worked as a secretary at the Foshay tower building. They accumulated friends in the Twin Cities metro and exchanged God parents, family with all. To this day I still have interaction with my God family.

Bruce and Marilyn Nichols – Wedding Duncombe Iowa

More background on Mom and Dad. Mom's Dad was in the Navy in WWII. Dad's dad was in the Army. Dad was in the Army in Germany post WWII. All of the Nichols men since the Nichols brothers of Nichols Iowa did service in the US military. The town of Nichols Iowa was founded around 1863.

Dad was the mayor of Alden and the American Legion Post Commander for years. I remember several years of getting the Memorial day poppies out to graves in western Freeborn County, Minnesota.

Both Mom and Dad's religion was Catholic. There was no Catholic church in Alden. The nearest ones were roughly ten miles away east and west. Some Catholics in Alden went to Wells and some went to Albert Lea for church.

Picture courtesy of Peoble Divers / Peoble Photography, Albert Lea Minnesota

I thought the picture above would be good for this story. It is me in 6th Grade. Mom always wanted us kids to dress very good for school pictures. For some reason she was not real happy with this picture. I guess I did my best that year for pictures! It covered both Alden and Conger, the two little towns that made up the rural school.

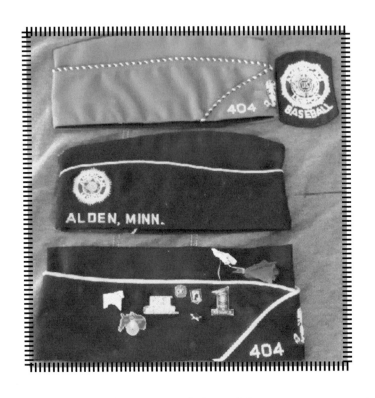

American Legion baseball was a big part of the Alden community in the summer and still is to this date. Dad was the commander for several years. My part was playing for the baseball team along with kids from Alden, Conger, and Freeborn. I can remember helping Dad out with putting poppies on graves in western Freeborn county. I loved both high school baseball and American Legion baseball. In high school most of the games were against small conference teams in southern Minnesota. It had the name Border Conference – a fitting name as the schools were along the Iowa border.

Legion ball was different in that Alden was able to play any size post. We played much larger posts throughout south and south eastern Minnesota. We always had good teams in my time playing so the larger post distinction really did not really come in to play.

As baseball is a background theme it still continues to be a pastime in my life. I have visited many professional games around the country. Some may see the game as too slow. I find a great throw in the hole at short for an out as equal to a blast of a home run.

This is the 1983 Alden American Legion baseball team. Picture setting is Tink field in Waseca Minnesota.

The Alden American Legion team consisted of players from the towns of Alden, Conger, and Freeborn. A subset of the Alden Conger High School and Freeborn High School baseball teams comprised the squad. The teams from both schools were usually pretty good. Being in a rural area a lot of kids needed to work on farms for the summer and did not have time for "ball". The rest of that had the time enjoyed a game most of us grow up with.

The next picture is the Alden Conger baseball team photo of 1984. Most of the older members went to play American Legion ball and the younger ones in ninth grade went on to play JR high equivalent leagues around Albert Lea Minnesota.

Coach Pierce (upper right) and the 1984 Alden-Conger HS Baseball team. I am next to coach. The team went undefeated in conference that year.

Sports were big with the Nichols family. My brother Tom, and identical twin, had unlimited sports our whole life. We played on most teams together. It ran from football, wrestling, to baseball. I would have played golf but the Minnesota state league would not allow two sports in the same time. Both Tom and myself excelled in all sports. My claim to fame was a long state run in wrestling one year. That said we couldn't get enough. We even would try to root for the Vikings at the end of every year to just be disappointed again (it stands to this day).

Baseball was a sport we played together. It was softball in later years. My time with him was great all through life. A portion is documented in my book "Being a Twin. " We played ball together and were on some really good teams. In ninth grade our team won an area championship. We played against teams from Albert Lea and Austin Minnesota. In high school we either won or were second for all conference leagues. Neil Pierce was the High School coach. Ken Anderson was the American Legion coach.

Snapshot of gloves. Elementary, Jounior High, Senior High.

CHAPTER

3

THE INCIDENT

Up until now in the book is a short background of relevant information. The next section will be as much as I can describe on the incident. The setting is an American Legion baseball game. It was Alden versus Mankato in Mankato Minnesota. The Alden team consisted of kids from the Alden Conger school and the Freeborn school. Most already knew each other and got along well as a team.

The "incident" happened to be an American Legion baseball game in Mankato Minnesota in the summer of 1983. My Alden team played Mankato. The day was sunny and windy. The game was close. I believe the score was 1-1 before the game was suspended in the last inning. I will get to that soon.

I made it to first base on either a base hit or a walk. I attempted to steal second base. Our team was full of very fast players. Stealing second after a hit was usually a given. As I was running I could see the ball skipping in to center field below the glove of the second baseman as I was getting to slide feet first. It was going to be an easy stolen base.

The next instance is pretty fuzzy but I still remembered. The second baseman kept his knee down and I basically slid in to it. I was still going pretty fast. There impact had his knee going in to my stomach and then up under the rib cage. I landed on my back on the bag and instinctively tried to sit up. I couldn't. At that point I just remember trying to take a grasped of air but I couldn't.

I only remember just falling backward. That is when the darkness occurred. I was out.

At that point in what I guess would be unconsionceness. The feeling was I was down but still felt awake. The following part is a description of what I saw next.

My first instinct was to get up. I couldn't. It felt likea heavy blanket on me which kept getting heavier and heavier. Something was definitely not right. I started yelling "help me". I did this through the rest of "dark" time.

Next I saw images of family. Tom, Mom, and Dad. It was like looking at a caresell with their faces rotating around. This continued for a while when suddenly he images started to speed up faster and faster. It got to the point everything was spinning faster and faster. I was still yelling for help. It was going so fast for the first time I had the feeling "uh oh, now I must be toast."

During this spinning sensation the background seemed dark with family faces only visible.

Then it stopped. The view became calm and very vivid. Just like game day it was nice and sunny but little or no wind. I was sitting or laying on the side of a small creek elevated a little up the hill. There was a small grove of trees on the other side. It felt like I was looking west as the Sun was coming through the trees. The creek seem shallow and had a light water flow.

Then the second of what seemed to "toast" happened. Once again the setting was tranquil. I still thought I was out so kept yelling for help. What is going on now. Unlike the previous visions the scene was very vivid.

At that point I see movement on the other side of the creek. Some one was walking down toward the creek at a pace they were going to walk across. Then I noticed the person. It was Jesus. I figured now I really am done. As he stepped in to the creek every thing stopped or just seemed like an instant transition.

That is when my eyes opened and the picture seemed normal again. Wow. I was still alive. I was still laying right on the base. All I could see was 15 to 20 sets of feet in my face. The wind was blowing in to my eyes as they shuffled. My instinct was to sit up. We have a game to continue.

With all the players around me something was wrong. How did they get here so quick. It was at least the whole Alden team and coaches. Then I noticed two ambulances in the outfield. Something bad happened.

The first thing I did was ask a fellow player "Didn't you hear my screams for help?" He just said "No".

The time I was out seemed only like 30 to 60 seconds. The time I was out I was given some info of everyone watching. The info came in bits and pieces over the next few days. No one wanted to discuss much about it. I don't blame them. My friend Jay Jensen said I turned blue. I was told someone tried to check vitals and offered there was no breathing or heart beat. I guess coach Ken Anderson tried to do CPR but didn't really know how and just punched me in the chest. I guess a dad of the Mankato team walked out and just walked away.

In hindsight I am sure everyone their just witnessed a very freak moment. I was ready to just play ball but the game was already called. Mankato was already schedule to visit Alden in the next weekend. Game was suspended to be finshed in a week.

I felt fine but with the ambulances already waiting an executive decision was made to go the hospital and just make sure things were ok. I remember going in to what I guess was some form of urgent care. I still felt ok. There a set of three nurses one by one asking me the same set of about 25 questions with the last one "do you feel nautious?". No, No, and on and on. I wondered the value of all this. I just wanted to go home at that point.

Finally the Doc showed up and chatted a little. He just felt for bruises and said before I get let go he wanted a body scan of my midsection. Once the nurses wheeled me in the the scan room then I felt it come on. The nautious question. I told the closest nurse "I am going to puke" and I did. Luckily she was able to grab a pan for me to throw up in to.

They did the body scan and I was let go with Mom. I was happy to get home. I was ok, felt ok, and there would be more ball to play. Lots of time left in the summer.

The next few pages are of the incident's medical records. The setting of course is Mankato Minnesota. The hospital name is St. Joseph, which is now part of the Mayo Clinic network in southern Minnesota. There are written details of this and some very hard to read. Sorry. The date noted is 6-23-84. The "Reason For Call" is "Baseball Player Is Down".

There is also a lot of medical notes. Some are hard to read and I don't understand many of them. The one that is of particular interest is "INVOLVED IN BASEBALL ACC, SLIDING IN TO BASE. WAS STRUCK IN CHEST – (MIDSTERNAL). LOSS OF CONSC. BYSTAND STATE WAS NOT BREATHING FOR APPROX 30 SECONDS".

The records of the hospital and emergency records follow.

MAYO CLINIC

Mayo Clinic
200 First Street SW
Rochester, MN 55905

February 05, 2019

Nichols,Timothy J.

RE: Request for Records of: Mr. Timothy J. Nichols
        Date of Birth: 8/25/1965
        Date request received: 1/31/2019
        Release ID: 19698578

Dear Nichols,Timothy J.,

In response to your recent request for medical records, enclosed is a copy of the requested information regarding care and treatment from Mayo Clinic Health System, Minnesota. You may see duplication of immunizations and other notes and results due to the integration of historical records into the new, single Mayo Clinic electronic health record.

Some documents may not have been finalized yet by the provider and could be subject to change. These copies are the most current version of the medical record as of the date and time printed.

Should you have any questions, you may contact us at 507-594-2621, Monday through Friday, 8:00 a.m. until 5:00 p.m., or write to the address above, attention Health Information Management Services-Release of Information.

Sincerely,

Release of Information
Health Information Management Services

Company: GOLD CROSS   **Reason for call:** BASEBALL   PLAYER DOWN

Crew: 241-247-254

Date: 6-23-84   **Call #** 00717-1   507/874-3622

Location: MSU - STADIUM + WARREN   DOB 8-25-65

Destination: St. JOES ER

Name: TIM NICHOLS

Address: 264 POWERS AVE

ALDEN, MN 56009

First responder: Dr. MANAHAN

Pt. M.D.:   **Monitor M.D./R.N.:**   **Receiving M.D./R.N.:**   **I Refuse Treatment/Transportation**

	LEVEL OF CONSCIOUSNESS	MENTAL STATUS	PUPILS	TIME	Medications: TYPE/DOSE
AGE 18	☒ Alert ☐ Reacts To Pain	☒ Oriented	R L ☐☐ Constricted		O₂
WT. 160	☐ Drowsy ☐ Unresponsive	☐ Disoriented	☐☐ Dilated		N/A
SEX M	☐ Reacts To Voice ☐ Deteriorated Enroute		☐☐ Reacts ☐☐ Unreactive		

Chief Complaint Chest PAIN from injury

History of Present Illness/Injury INVOLVED IN BASEBALL ACC. SLIDING INTO BASE. WAS STRUCK IN CHEST (MIDSTERNAL). LOSS OF CONSC. BYSTANDERS STATE WAS NOT BREATHING FOR APPROX 30 SECONDS. Dr. MANAHAN FOUND HIM 1 minute LATER ALERT + ORIENTED X3 CYANOSIS NOTED before Dr. MANAHANS ARRIVAL. ☐ APPARENT SEIZURE ACTIVITY

Past History Allergies/Meds. ALLG - Ø
MEDS - Ø
MED Hx - Ø

Physical Exam and Treatment FOUND LYING ON (R) SIDE OF BODY ALERT + ORIENTED X3. C/O MID STERNAL chest PAIN. Site shows NO BRUISING OR DEFORMITY. DENIES PAIN IN chest REGION AND THROUGHOUT BODY. GOOD LUNG SOUNDS BILATERALLY. SKIN COLOR GOOD, WARM + DRY. GOOD EQUAL STRONG MOVEMENTS IN ALL EXTREMITIES. SCOOP stretcher to AMBULANCE → TRANSPORT S JOES ER CODE I EKG - NSR Ē Ø ECTOPY

Other: **Signature:**

Time	B/P	Pulse	Resp.	Time-Military Called	1648	Odometer Start	
4:53	104/58	92	16	Enroute	1648	At Scene	04
5:00	108/60	92	16	Ar Scene	1653	At Hosp	06
				Lv Scene	1704		
				Ar Hosp	1711		
				In Service	1716		

TREATMENTS
☐ Oral Airway
☐ Esophageal Airway
☐ Endotracheal Airway

☐ Oxygen   ☐ CPR
☐ Limb Splints   ☐ Citizen CPR
☐ Traction Splint   ☐ Defibrillation
☒ Spine Board   ☐ Pulmonary Resuscitation
☐ Cervical Collar
☐ I.V. Fluids   ☐ Suction
☐ Medications   ☐ MAST
☐ Obstetrical   ☒ EKG
☐ Restraints   ☐ Follow-up

HE 00251-04 8/83

IMMANUEL-ST. JOSEPH'S HOSPITAL 149   EMERGENCY DEPARTMENT RECORD

ACCT #	10206001		REF. MD			ATTEND. MD	
DATE	10-23-84	TIME 5:14	M	PRIVATE MD Schmitt-Ald		ER MD Clochieux	
LAST NAME	Nichols,	FIRST Timothy	MIDDLE J.		AGE 18	DOB 3-25-65	
ADDRESS		CITY,	STATE			MED REC. NO.	

TIME	BP R / L	T	P	R	CHRONIC DISEASES/OPERATIONS:	none / none.
5:15p	128/80		76	22	CURRENT MEDS:	
5:55p	116/84		80			none
6p	124/82				ALLERGIES:	NKA
4:?p	118/80		80		TETANUS TOXOID:	PERSONAL EFFECTS:

DENTURES: CONTACTS   GLASSES

TIME	MEDICATION/TREATMENT	INIT	NURSES NOTES:

Problem: chest injury
c̄ Pt was brought to ED by Gold Cross
amb on a scoop stretcher —
was trying to steal 2nd base when
he collided w̄ another player, striking
his chest on other player's knee.
Was apparently knocked out briefly —
apnea < 30 sec. — on arrival to ED
pt is alert & oriented, remembers
colliding c̄ other player — denies
any discomfort at this time —
no contusions seen — resp. are clear

Vomited x 2 in x-ray dept —
has some diaphor now.
Feels better p̄ x-ray — asking to go home.
                                                          K Reimer RN

DR NOTIFIED

PHYSICIAN NOTES:
Skull PA + Lat
c spine PA + Lat
     nose/orbit

18 your playing baseball was struck in epigastrium c̄ sternal area by knee of
second baseman. Had wind knocked out. Also question of neck c̄ closed head injury
Difficulty breathing for several minutes. No weakness or hemoptysis.
Exam: A x 2 O x 3   PERRLA, EOMI, discs sharp. Cr nn II – XII intact.
    DTR's normal motor/sensory exam normal. Neck supple non tender
    Skull – no contusions or bruises. Chest – tender over xyphoid process
    in epigastrium. Abd supple non tender. No costovert. No rebound.
    Spleen tip palpable – non tender. Musculoskeletal exam normal. Rectal exam negative
    Skull, cervical spine, CXR: Abd to all negative.   Stools here ⊖
Discussed head injury sheet c̄ mother as well as precautions concerning abdominal
injury including nausea/bloated, drowsiness, or bloody sputum.
    to Dr Schmitt   Blood drawn to abdomen.
FOLLOWUP INSTRUCT. TO PT. AND/OR SIGNIFICANT OTHER | DIAGNOSIS
DISP disch   TIME 7:30p.   R Clochieux   MD
                                                      PHYSICIAN

SEND WHITE COPY TO MEDICAL RECORDS — YELLOW COPY TO ATTENDING DOCTOR — PINK COPY TO PRIVATE DOCTOR AND GOLD
COPY TO EMERGENCY DEPARTMENT.

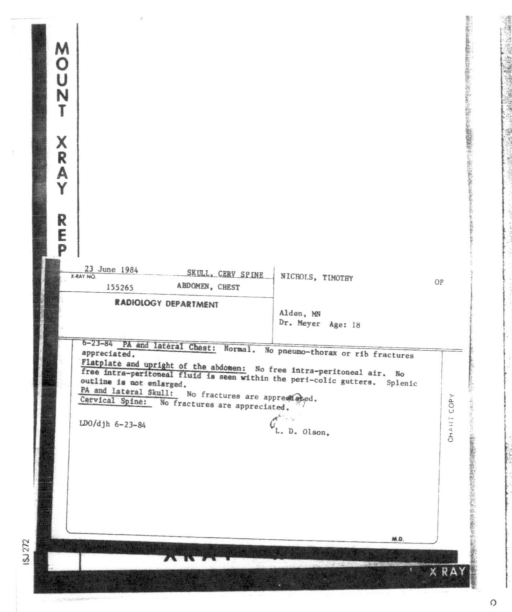

23 June 1984   SKULL, CERV SPINE   NICHOLS, TIMOTHY   OP

X-RAY NO.

155265   ABDOMEN, CHEST

RADIOLOGY DEPARTMENT

Alden, MN
Dr. Meyer   Age: 18

6-23-84 <u>PA and lateral Chest:</u> Normal. No pneumo-thorax or rib fractures appreciated.

<u>Flatplate and upright of the abdomen:</u> No free intra-peritoneal air. No free intra-peritoneal fluid is seen within the peri-colic gutters. Splenic outline is not enlarged.

<u>PA and lateral Skull:</u> No fractures are appreciated.

<u>Cervical Spine:</u> No fractures are appreciated.

LDO/djh 6-23-84

L. D. Olson.

M.D.

ISJ 272

X RAY

To this day of writing this book I have rarely discussed this incident. After all I was now alive and normal life just continues.

The Mankato team came to Alden to finish the suspended game and then play an already scheduled game. The first game started off with me at second base. While I walked to the bag the Mankato second baseman started walking to me. I didn't know what to think. Could he be pissed off about my being knocked out or maybe being a "faker" and made him look bad? No. He just offered he was sorry for his part in it. I can't image what he went through for a whole week. I just told him with a smile "It's ok. Just don't do it again.". He smiled and I could tell felt some sort of relief.

1984 Alden-Conger Senior High School Graduation Picture

Picture courtesy of Peoble Divers / Peoble Photography, Albert Lea Minnesota

CHAPTER

4

WHAT TO TAKE OF THIS – MY THOUGHTS

The next section is my attempt at some explanations of this incident. I have my own thoughts and some research from some related near death bodies of work. Explanations of this run the gammit of many ideas. As I mention at the beginning of the book the intention for the book was to be for readers interested in this kind of experience and any researchers looking for any more replications to further their own knowledge base.

Being a software engineer my whole career I thought of this from the view of a computer itself. Think of it as a rationale of how a computer operates and similar concepts or explanations of near death experience. Could the visions I was seeing those that were most in my mind at the time? Would they be the computer equivalent of RAM or some other storage. Some computer systems have a concept of saving storage on the concept of system shutdown. The data being processed as it is being saved is "seen" for processing by the CPU at shutdown. Could the visions I was seeing be the equivalent here.

My visions of family and Jesus may have been the most important things to process while I was passed out. Storage memory passing through the CPU on the way to system shutdown. In addition could the "actions" of the a heavy blanket coming over me and my shouts for help a standard reaction banked in the mind on how to react to this situation. The same goes for the thoughts of where I was about to be dead. It could all be a part of the system being shutdown while doing final processing. It reminds me of people in movies, just before death can scratch out one last phrase while conscious knowing they are about to die.

But why only see family and Jesus? Sports and sports event memories were big in my mind. Coaches, teachers, friends, extended family, the person running the cash register at the gas station buying the last can of coke there. Why not any visions of this and you could think of thousands more that could have been banked and available to be "seen"? Why not the face of the second baseman just before impact?

Why the vision of Jesus just before coming back? The Church was pretty standard operation. The family was your run of the mill Catholic family. Was it an attempt to pray at death and Jesus would be the next person to be seen? Again, these are some ideas I have on all of this.

Was I dead? My classmate Jay Jensen said my body turned to the color of blue. That would explain the lack of oxygen in the blood. Along with that, and I don't remember who offered it, supposedly others checked for lack of breathing and lack of a pulse.

The time gap of my sense of 30 to 60 seconds of "awareness" doesn't exactly match the full length of time I was out. From an interview with Jay Jensen he thought it was roughly 2 minutes before it was realized something was wrong. Throw in a couple more to call for an ambulance. Then add in how long it would take for the ambulance to arrive at the scene. In my estimization it was at least 5 minutes. That would be time of impact to my eyes opening.

CHAPTER

5

OTHER WRITING ON NDEs

There is a wide range of material on this subject. The work of John C. Hagan III is good material of his own and other work related to the subject. The book is The *Science of NEAR-DEATH EXPERIENCES*. It contains links to many other science and related knowledge and studies on this subject.

In Hagaan 's Forward I found the following interesting:

The clinical situation is usually straightforward… Interpreting such an experience should be left to the patient. In particular, attempting to explain near-eath experiences neurophysiologically as hallucinations induced by oxygen deprivation to the brain typically alienates patients.

I never thought about discussing my incident until now. Not even with immediate family. For myself it has taken time to even bring this up. My hope is this work can be input for both science and religion.

I disagree of course with Hagan III on whether physicians have a preferred account of NDE s. With my background in computer engineering and medical product development, I believe I may be an objective observer AND actual witness to this - myself. I can still account the short time of memory of when this happened.

Positive effects of Near Death experience.

Hagan III refers to positive effects of near death experience (NDE). He states *NDEs can permanently and dramatically alter the individual experiencer's attitudes, beliefs, and failures. The literature on the after effects of NDEs has focused on the beneficial personal transformations that often follow. A recent review of research into the characteristic changes following NDEs fount the most commonly reported to be loss of fear of death; strengthened belief in life after death ; feeling specially favored by God; a new sense of purpose of mission; hieightened self-esteem; increased compassion and lof for others; lessened concern for material gain, recognition, or status; greater desire to serve others; increased ability to express feelings; greater appreciation of, and zest for, life; increased focus on the present; deeper religious faith or heithtened spirituality; search for knowledge; and greater appreciation for nature. (6 Hagan). These aftereffects have been corroborated by interviews with near-death experiencers' significant others and by long-term longitudinal studies(17 Hagan).*

That happened with me. It is more of a reflection at this point in my life. Could it have helped me to grow and strive afterwords? Maybe. The acquisition for knowledge of anything is there. The goal to lead when I can is there. The second base incident was a scare but it did not hold me back from playing sports again. It just happened. Life moves on. I was happy to be alive and with friends and family. That said the memory continues to this day.

More NDE background. Bestemam, in My Journey to Heaven, also cites Moody, and cites seeing heaven and talking to Peter (Bestman Intro). The recollection described sounds were vivid. This was similar to my vivid scene of Jesus.

What can be made of these scenes? For myself it was seeing my family and then Jesus, in that specific order. Was the computer shutting down? That is the challenge of answering this, an age old question.

If we take a step back on people that know they will die soon but scribe beautiful works to others that are close I will point to Henry Scott Holland, who was a "pastor" in the mid 1800s. His Words follow in a picture on the next page.

Death is nothing at all. It does not count. I have only slipped away into the next room. Nothing has happened. Everything remains exactly as it was. I am I, and you are you, and the old life that we lived so fondly together is untouched, unchanged. Whatever we were to each other, that we are still. Call me by the old familiar name. Speak of me in the easy way which you always used. Put no difference into your tone. Wear no forced air of solemnity or sorrow. Laugh as we always laughed at the little jokes that we enjoyed together. Play, smile, think of me, pray for me. Let my name be ever the household word that it always was. Let it be spoken without an effort, without the ghost of a shadow upon it. Life means all that it ever meant. It is the same as it ever was. There is absolute and unbroken continuity. What is this death but a negligible accident? Why should I be out of mind because I am out of sight? I am but waiting for you, for an interval, some-where very near, just round the corner. All is well.

All is well.

Good words. This is obviously conscientious thought with the knowledge of knowing you are about to die soon. It is passing words to others. Meaningful words to others. The point of bringing this up is it may be another link of the mind knowing death is near. There is coherence in his thoughts. It talks about ghosts (religion), close ones (family and friends), and scribing he will be there "just round the corner" (after life). Also, a sign of care for close ones, "All is well". So what do we take of this? Do very wise words come when death is near?

Almost every sentence in his piece can have multiple meanings and thoughts for each ones memories in their own life. It covers now, immediately now, close to death, death, and after death and including a friendship and closeness with all. Now and later.

Back to NDEs

Long et al also cites there is no known explanation of NDE in EVIDENCE of the AFTERLIFE:

"There is no widely accepted definition of near-death experience. The NDERF study took a straightforward approach by defining both the near death and experience components of near-death experience. I considered individuals to be "near death" if they were so physically compromised that they would die if their condition did not improve. The NDErs studied were generally unconscious and often apparently clinically dead, with absence of heartbeat and breathing. The "experience" had to occur at the time they were near death. Also, the experience had to be lucid, to exclude description of only fragmentary and disorganized memory".

NDERF stands for Near Death Experience Research Foundation – NDERF.ORG.

Long's assertion that scenes are vivid close to the time of death fall in line with mine. Although the first part of the experience was rather blury with scenes of family the last one of seeing Jesus was a perfect day. It was serene.

In regards to the Jesus vision it may relate to Sigmund, in MY TIME IN HEAVEN. In my visions Jesus did not speak to me but rather the vision stopped and I awoke as he was crossing the creek to me. Sigmand refers to his instance with a message from Jesus in Chapter 21 titled "YOU ARE GOING BACK".

Jesus said, "You are going back." I sighed, and Jesus rebuked me. "The will of My Father is never grievous. Stand to your feet. You must go back. You will come back to heaven. You will have angelic visits," He said. Then, Jesus hugged me.

Suddenly, my body was full of pain. There was a sheet over my face. I could feel my bones knitting together; I was being healed. I heard a voice say, "He's been dead all these hours."

I could feel my left wrist where the bone had been protruding ---I could feel it popping into place and healing up.

"It is about time to embalm him."

I remember sitting up and saying, "I ain't dead yet."

"You are going back" is similar to me seeing Jesus just before my eyes opened. "I ain't dead yet" is similar to how I felt lying on second base. My first thoughts were simply hey I am still alive, I seem ok still, lets finish the ball game.

CHAPTER 6

CONCLUSION

Having a near death experience is something I have had a hard time discussing with family and friends. I don't want people to think this something made up or a dream. It wasn't. I put the hospital records for back up of this. As with many of the authors I read on NDE, the range of interpretation of the events vary. How can you quantify the solution to this? I don't think you can but appreciation is due to those who take the effort to put rational thought and study behind things that are irrational.

I will go back to the computer analogy here. It is what I have done and I am very familiar with it. Near Death Experience comes in many shapes and forms. A common theme in writings is family and religion. Is family and religion in RAM while more thought full memory in hard drive storage – always there when needed? In my humble observation there is no binary explanation for this type of experience. I believe all can be correct. I am a witness to this.

My sample size is 1 but hopefully others can use it for the future. That is my story and I stick to it! 2nd Base, I never thought an incident would have me writing about this years later. I hope the insight is helpful to all of you. Thank you.

The Author Credentials

Alden-Conger High School, Valedictorian, Alden Minnesota 1984

University of Wisconsin-Stout, Menomonie, Wisconsin, Applied Mathematics, 1988.

University of St. Thomas, St. Paul Minnesota, Masters in Business Administration (MBA), 1997.

US Patents

7,039,810 Method and apparatus to secure data from medical device systems

6,961,448 User authentication in medical device systems

6,363,282 Apparatus and method to automate remote software updates

6,266,566 Waveform normalization in a medical device

Book: Being a Twin by Timothy Nichols, ISBN 9781524675738.

Previous work: IBM, Poughkeepsie New York and Rochester Minnesota.

Medtronic, Minneapolis Minnesota

NOTES

Hagan III, John C. M.D. (2017), *The Science of NEAR-DEATH EXPERIENCE*, ISBN 978-0-8262-2103-2

Moody JR.,Raymond A. (1975) M.D. *Life After Life*, ISBN 978-0-06-242890-5

Besteman, Marvin J. (2012) *My Journey to Heaven*, ISBN 978-0-8007-2122-0

Long, Jeffrey M.D., Perry, (2010) *EVIDENCE of the AFTERLIFE*, ISBN 978-0-06-145257-4

Nichols, Timothy (2017), *Being a Twin*, ISBN 978-1-52467573-8

Sigmund, Richard (1973, 1978, 1984) *MY TIME IN HEAVEN: A True Story of Dying and Coming Back*, ISBN 978-1-60374-123-1

About The Author

Tim Nichols has been a author of another family related book called "Being a Twin". More information needs to be put here like HS, College, Kids, Career, etc. Tim is the inventor of four US Patents in the areas of computer and medical technology and has received many internal company awards from IBM and Medtronic.

Printed in the United States
By Bookmasters